STEVE McQUEEN

A Life in Pictures   Edited by Yann-Brice Dherbier

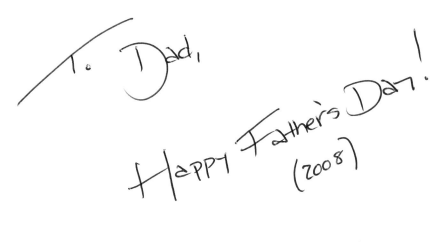

To Dad,

Happy Father's Day!
(2008)

all my love,

Nic xxx

First published in Great Britain in 2008 by Pavilion Books

An imprint of Anova Books Company Ltd

10 Southcombe Street, London, W14 0RA

© Anova Books Company Ltd, 2008

First published in France in 2007 by YB Éditions

Text © Axelle Emden, 2007

Additional text © Yann-Brice Dherbier, 2007

Cover photography © Roger-Viollet

Translation © Pavilion Books

Layout: Renaud Sauteret (sauteret@free.fr)

Editor (UK): Kate Burkhalter

Translator: JMS Publishing

ISBN 978 1 862058 14 9

Printed and bound by EBS, Italy

Reproduction by Gorne, Paris

10 9 8 7 6 5 4 3 2 1

www.anovabooks.com

STEVE McQUEEN

A Life in Pictures   Edited by Yann-Brice Dherbier

Steve Mc Queen

STEVE McQUEEN

A lost childhood: Missouri, Indiana and California (1930–42)

Terence Steven McQueen was born on 24 March 1930 in Beech Grove, a small town in Indiana. His parents were Bill McQueen and Julia Ann Crawford, known as Julian. The young Steven had a very tough childhood, marked by the departure of his father, who took off soon after his birth.

Julian was a runaway who had left her home in Slater, Missouri for the city. A year later, aged 21, she met Bill, an ex-aviator and former stunt-pilot who had served in the Navy. Bill, known as 'Red', came from a military family whose ancestors, of Scottish origin, had settled in the United States in the 1750s. Julian's family was Catholic. A year after meeting Bill, Julian gave birth to a son and shortly after took Bill's surname, although it's unlikely they ever got married. Was Steve's birth planned? It is difficult to say whether Julian and Bill would have wanted a child. Julian drank, while Bill had been addicted to morphine since receiving treatment for heart trouble in 1928. Shattered by morphine before he was 30, Bill left Julian and Steven in a hotel six months after his son's birth. He came back several weeks later, begging Julian to forgive him, but she showed him the door.

Steve McQueen had only unhappy memories of his childhood. 'My life was booby-trapped before I was born,' he would say later. Throughout his life, he would quote Shakespeare's *The Merchant of Venice* as an echo of his early years – 'The sins of the father are to be laid upon the children' (Act III, sc.V, l. 1) – sometimes substituting the word 'mother' in the original quotation.

Born in poverty, the young Steven was brought up in insecurity; violent 'stepfathers' and arguments at home filled his daily life. His mother became a semi-prostitute, some weeks bringing home three, four or even five men. Steven began to hate her even more than he hated the father he had never known. If he wasn't being shouted at by the men taking advantage of his mother, it was Julian who shouted at her son. The child quickly withdrew into solitude and soon he went home only to sleep. Many years later, Steve told his wife, Neile, that his infancy was 'the worst shit you could imagine'. Then Julian decided to leave her son with her uncle, who had a farm in her home town of Slater, Missouri. Steven was thus partly brought up by his Uncle Claude and throughout his life never forgave his mother for inflicting this second abandonment on him.

Steven was a pale child with light eyes, who spoke to no one and had serious learning difficulties. Dyslexia was later diagnosed, along with an infection contracted at the end of the 1930s that permanently damaged his left ear. Neglected by his mother, he spent some time in the care of this uncle, a brutal, opportunistic farmer. At the age of nine, he went to live with his mother again, in Indianapolis, but they did not get on well. A marginal child, he retained that feeling of being different all his life, damaged by never knowing his father and knowing his mother so little.

During this deprived and difficult childhood, the cinema seemed like magic. Steve McQueen was a child of the 1930s, the years that saw the emergence of films committed to dealing with society's ills, as well as gangster movies, an equal reflection of those troubled times. It's not surprising to learn that young Steve was fascinated by John Ford's *The Grapes of Wrath*, which came out in 1940. Steve grew up on sad movies inspired by the misery of the Depression, but there was also escapism: *Wuthering Heights*, *The Wizard of Oz* and westerns like *Billy the Kid*, *Cavalier of the West* and *Stagecoach* filled the screens. *Gone with the Wind*, *Mrs Miniver* and *Casablanca* fascinated the young Steven, who particularly admired Bogart after seeing him in *High Sierra*: 'He was the master and always will be,' he said of 'Bogie' in 1972. John Wayne and Gary Cooper were also big stars.

Adventure films also flourished during the period, starring Errol Flynn, or Johnny Weissmuller as Tarzan. Escapist cinema also included musical comedy with stars such as Ginger Rogers and Fred Astaire, Maurice Chevalier and Jeannette MacDonald. Steve McQueen grew up in Hollywood's golden age; according to S.N. Berman, during the 1940s 'Hollywood became a kind of Athens. It was as crowded with artists as Renaissance Florence.'

Steven was barely adolescent but he was already uncontrollable, hanging out with gangs in Indianapolis. Later on, he would sometimes compare these years to Fellini's *I Vitelloni*. 'That film sums up the sort of kids we were at that time,' he used to say. In 1940, Julian again sent her son home to Slater.

He went back to living with his Uncle Claude, an alcoholic with a violent temper who was then living with Eva, an ex-burlesque dancer from St Louis, half his age. Steven sometimes saw his grandfather who lived nearby and who was then in the terminal stages of cancer. His grandmother had become a religious fanatic and was suffering from dementia – on some days she could hardly recognize her grandson. Julian never visited her son or her parents. The boy lived here for some time, in an isolation in which nobody took care of a 12-year old child who was already in chronic depression and family breakdown. 'When a kid doesn't have any love when he's small,' he explained later, 'he begins to wonder if he's good enough. My mother didn't love me, and I didn't have a father. I thought 'Well, I must not be any good.' So, then you go out and try to prove yourself, and I always did things that other people wouldn't do. Dangerous things. I was always kind of a coward until I had to prove it to myself.'

From adolescent nightmares to the brink of liberty: from Los Angeles to New York (1942–51)

In 1942, Julian, by now married to a man called Berri (Steve could never remember his surname), took her son back, this time to live in California. When Steven arrived in Los Angeles, he said later, he thought he'd landed on Mars. There, he was faced with a new, violent stepfather who frequently threatened to throw them both out if they didn't get jobs. One evening the child decided to write a letter to his Uncle Claude and began by describing his daily life in fractured English filled with spelling mistakes. At the end of the letter it was possible to decipher a clumsy 'Help'. But the SOS never reached its destination and Berri punished Steven for his inadequate writing. At Christmas, Steven was arrested for theft. He continued to hang out with gangs, this time in Los Angeles; barely in his teens, he was already no stranger to violence, crime, the taunts of his schoolmates at his dyslexia, continual physical abuse and the rejection of being Catholic in a Protestant environment. He returned to Missouri, then went back to Los Angeles in 1944. Yet again, he led the life of a young delinquent. In February 1945, his mother and stepfather declared him legally 'incorrigible'. He was 14.

His mother then sent him to Boys Republic, a home for wayward boys. He ran away immediately but was soon caught. In this reform school in suburban Los Angeles, Steven learned discipline. He made his bed for the first time in his life, cleared the canteen table and in the afternoon worked in the laundry. Some biographies state that he was sexually assaulted during those years. He tried to escape four more times but in all spent 14 long months at Boys Republic.

By now, Julian had moved to New York and in 1946, having travelled all week by bus, Steven arrived in Manhattan on 22 April. It was another disaster: he found his mother a widow – Berri had died just as the couple were about to divorce – and Julian was now living with another man, Lukens. She did not welcome Steven, who learned yet again that he was not wanted.

Steven had nowhere to go, but he took advantage of all New York had to offer. He made a few dollars in pool tournaments, spent his evenings cruising around on his Vespa scooter and quickly made friends in night clubs and bars. One evening, after several drinks in a bar in Little Italy, two men got him to sign a piece of paper; he found he had signed up for the merchant navy. He set sail for Trinidad but jumped ship in Santo Domingo, where he worked in a brothel for some months before working his way through Texas and on up to Canada. In Ontario he called himself Steve for the first time. At last he was seeing the country. Next he drifted to North Carolina and the same year, 1946, worked as a driller, a logger and occasionally as a boxer.

In 1947 McQueen joined the Marines, serving as a mechanic for three years. His best friend at that time remembered: 'There was nobody better in the world to have on your side, and nobody worse to cross than McQueen.' Another friend from Camp Lejeune recalled: 'McQueen had a gift for mimicry.' Steve was a rebellious and sarcastic young man, amusing but always solitary, difficult to pin down but charming. He played a lot of poker and often sized up his opponents by the way they played, being known for not giving his opinion of a new recruit until he had played cards with him. He liked to win and remained a rebel; a friend recalled him 'reading his rights' – the right to drink, to get laid or to race bikes. He quickly became notorious for his insubordination.

He was posted to Virginia, then graduated to the Gun Factory in Washington DC. After yet another adverse report, his best friend asked what he planned to do next. Steve replied: 'As far as I can see, I got two choices. I could go on stage, or I could go to jail.' As his friend said, 'Most people's money would have been on the latter.' Many years later, Steve McQueen confided: 'I made films, and I wanted to be respected in the movie industry, but to tell the truth I'm not sure that acting is something for a grown man to be doing.'

Steve spent weeks on disciplinary work details where, among other things, he had to strip out a ship's boiler room, exposing him to high levels of asbestos. Despite his indiscipline, he could act heroically and during this period he saved five men from drowning when their transport sank. After three years in the US Marines, Steve returned to civilian life, driving a taxi in Washington before moving in 1950 to New York, where he worked as a docker and a barman. He lived in Greenwich Village, renting an apartment in a 'cold-water' building for $19 a month. He tried his hand at many trades – he drove a taxi, repaired televisions, delivered newspapers, played poker and worked as a bookie's runner. He even sold encyclopaedias and arranged flowers.

From acting studies to feature films (1951–63)

In June 1951, Steven signed up for acting lessons given by Sandford Meisner at the Neighborhood Playhouse. Meisner sensed that here was a candidate for the big screen: 'He was an original, both tough and childlike – as if he'd been through the ways but preserved a certain basic innocence. I accepted him at once.' The GI Bill and poker winnings paid for Steve's acting lessons and in his spare time he went bike racing on Long Island. In 1952, he started at New York's Actors Studio.

What was Steve McQueen like at this time? He was a man who hated getting up early in the morning; he was depressed for most of the day; after too many years of misery, he dreamed of fame and girls. At night he often stayed up late, thinking back over his life, although he had barely begun to live it; these long vigils often made him ill. Basically insecure, he was constantly at war with the world and at 21 the man nicknamed 'Bandito' thought life was an endurance test.

Steve McQueen joined the Actors Studio in the early 1950s. The cinema's golden age of the 1930s and 1940s was over; America was in the grip of McCarthyism and, to avoid problems, films known as 'runaway productions' were made outside Hollywood. Members of the Actors Studio disdained films of escapism and spectacle, instead advocating productions of psychological depth, dealing with human issues and social criticism. This school espoused a new method of direction and another, more introspective, way of acting. Marked by the training he had received in New York since 1951, McQueen belonged to this new generation of actors, that of Lee Strasberg and Elia Kazan who taught the Stanislavski method – a complete identification with the person or the situation, as opposed to the Hollywood method that tended to package scripts and characters with ready-made or up-and-coming stars. From those Actors Studio years came directors such as Sidney Lumet, but above all a generation of actors to which McQueen belonged; it included Elizabeth Taylor, Paul Newman, John Cassavetes, Jane Fonda, Warren Beatty, Dustin Hoffman and even Robert de Niro and Al Pacino, as well as James Dean, Marilyn Monroe and Marlon Brando.

Encouraged by this tuition, Steve McQueen made his debut on Broadway in 1955, in the play *A Hatful of Rain*. A year later he appeared in his first film, *Somebody Up There Likes Me*, starring Paul Newman and Pier Angeli and directed by Robert Wise, which many years later inspired the legendary *Rocky*. McQueen had a bit part for which he was paid $19 a day. In 1958 he appeared in *Never Love a Stranger*, directed by Robert Stevens, and in 1959 *The Great St Louis Bank Robbery*, directed by Charles Guggenheim and John Stix, but his roles were still small.

In 1957, at the age of 27, McQueen married the 21-year-old actress Neile Adams, with whom he would have two children – a daughter, Terry, who was born in Los Angeles two years later, on 5 June 1959, and a son, Chad, who was born on 28 December 1960, also in Los Angeles.

After several more small parts in films, in which he was still called Steven, McQueen landed a leading role in *The Blob*, directed by Irvin S. Yeaworth Jr. He opted for a fee of $3,000, rather than the offered 10 per cent profit participation. *The Blob* grossed $20 million.

Shortly afterwards Steve McQueen made an impression in *Never So Few* in 1959 and above all in *The Magnificent Seven* (1960), both directed by John Sturges. By now he was well-known, thanks to the TV series *Wanted Dead or Alive*, in which he starred as bounty hunter Josh Randall, a part he played from 1958 to 1961, providing him with a regular salary for three years. His character, Randall, was an ambivalent loner with a sawn-off Winchester shotgun. McQueen doubtless owed to the series his casting in *The Magnificent Seven*, as John Sturges wanted a strong, likeable character for his western. Desperate to get out of the TV series and to be in the film, Steve faked a car crash. It worked. *The Magnificent Seven* was inspired by Kurosawa's *Seven Samurai* and Steve McQueen shared billing with Charles Bronson, James Coburn, Horst Buchholz, Yul Brynner, Eli Wallach, Robert

Vaughn and Brad Dexter. From now on, violence and sexuality would be portrayed overtly in the cinema. The film was a hit and McQueen gave a remarkable performance. On screen, he was rebellious without boasting, disdainful without hatred, sexy without sentimentality.

His next film was *The Honeymoon Machine*, directed by Richard Thorpe in 1961. It was his first starring role and his first comedy, a genre he would later avoid. That was the year he founded Solar Inc., his own production company. His next movie was Don Siegel's *Hell is for Heroes*, in which he played a soldier before being cast as a pilot in Philip Leacock's *The War Lover* in 1962, starring as daredevil Capt. Buzz Rickson opposite Shirley Anne Field. But it was *The Great Escape* a year later, in 1963, that made Steve McQueen famous.

The Great Escape: the explosion (1963–5)

Director John Sturges played a significant part in the McQueen mythology – after *The Magnificent Seven*, which had launched the actor, he rocketed to fame for his role in *The Great Escape*. The film told the story of a group of English and American POWs in a Nazi prisoner-of-war camp who organize an ambitious escape. Sturges's film made an international star of Steve McQueen, thanks to his performance as a super-cool daredevil, a style the actor would adopt permanently. Starring alongside him were James Coburn and Charles Bronson, with whom he had filmed *The Magnificent Seven*. Always a risk-taker and true hothead, McQueen rose to all challenges, doing his own stunts on a 650cc Triumph motorcycle. His motorcycle leap across a 12-ft barbed-wire fence remains one of the most famous feats in action films of the time. 'Steve played suffering perfectly', recalled James Clavell, who worked on the film. *The Great Escape* was a huge international hit. It was nominated for Oscars and Golden Globes in 1964; Steve McQueen was runner-up in the Laurel Awards for Best Action Performance and won the award for Best Actor at Moscow's International Film Festival.

At 33, Steve McQueen emerged as a laid-back free spirit, the 'King of Cool'. It was the start of a movie career that would make him a huge star. A kind of arrogance, an assumed insouciance and a touch of insolence – the actor was the perfect rebel for the 1960s. McQueen belonged to the generation of James Dean and Marlon Brando; perpetually tormented by his difficult early years, he carried within him a rebelliousness that he knew how to exploit for the characters he played. With his timeless, relaxed elegance, Steve McQueen seduced his public through his raw charm and understated acting. Trained in the Actors Studio but independent of all schools, McQueen stripped all pretension from his acting, infusing his characters with a vitality that came from his behaviour. His acting was powerful and effortless, raw and complex. In some inexplicable way, McQueen appealed to cinema and television viewers all over the world.

The year 1963 was another significant one – after *The Great Escape*, Robert Mulligan, a director alert to the psychology of his characters, suggested to him a more nuanced role in *Love with the Proper Stranger*. 'For the first time in my life, when I look at a girl I feel I'm 14,' exclaims Rocky Papasano, played by McQueen. 'And even when I was 14, I didn't feel like this.' Steve soon fell for Natalie Wood and she was seduced both on screen and off, an adventure that quickly gained McQueen a reputation as a heartbreaker. 'When I think of the way I treated some women, I feel bad, I feel sick,' he would say later. For now, on screen, Steve McQueen and Natalie Wood transcended their star status to play ordinary people, powerfully. The following year the film gained five Oscar nominations but McQueen was not among them. He was nominated for a Golden Globe award, as was Natalie Wood, but neither won.

The same year, he also made *Soldier in the Rain*, directed by Ralph Nelson, for which his fee was $300,000 plus a percentage of the film's gross. Two years later, he worked again with Robert Mulligan on *Baby, the Rain Must Fall*, in which he gave a powerful performance as a conman turned musician. McQueen's portrayal of the broken-down, vulnerable Henry Thomas was one of his most intense. Mulligan enjoyed working with Steve: 'McQueen had great vitality,' he recalled. 'He had a sort of theatrical daring, the same nerve that he had when behind the wheel of his racing car. He never left it in the dressing-room when he went on the set.' The future director of *Summer of '42* (1971) knew how to showcase McQueen's physical presence while offering him genuine roles. McQueen gave a poignant performance as a prisoner on remand at the mercy of the neighbouring sheriff. His interpretation is often described as his most masterly portrayal – one that came closest to his own damaged personality, which he tried so hard to conceal.

His next adventure was to take part in a motorcycle competition in Erfurt, Germany, riding a Triumph 500cc. In 1964, he decided to take 18 months off work to devote himself to motor racing and motorcycles. 'I decided to be an actor so that I wouldn't be jerked around 40 hours a week,' he said. 'But I haven't got away from it, since I now work 72 hours a week. Go figure…' So he took a break to devote himself to his second passion. 'An actor is a puppet, manipulated by a dozen people,' McQueen said. 'Motor racing is more dignified. But it needs the same absolute concentration. You have to dig deep within yourself and crawl over a lot of broken glass.' During his sporting break, he was nominated for another Golden Globe for his performance in *Love with the Proper Stranger*.

The paths of glory: from Cincinnati to *Bullitt* (1965–9)

After *Baby, the Rain Must Fall*, Steve played *The Cincinnati Kid* in 1965, directed by Norman Jewison, who had been brought in to replace Sam Peckinpah. Jewison tore up the script and decided to focus the film around the world of poker.

McQueen had no problem playing a seasoned poker player. 'After the game, I'll be The Man. I'll be the best there is. People will sit down at the table with you, just so they can say they played with The Man. And that's what I'm gonna be.' During the 1960s and in the films he made in those years, Steve McQueen became The Man, the King of Cool, and that's the way he stayed. But he had rivals – Paul Newman for one, as he saw it. When *The Cincinnati Kid* was released, McQueen hated and never understood the inevitable comparisons with Newman's character in *The Hustler*.

In 1966 he made *Nevada Smith* with Henry Hathaway. He was cast as Max Sand, a young man whose parents are murdered. When he finds their tortured and mutilated bodies, he is determined to find and kill their murderers. Armed with this one obsession, he sets out to track them down. The 36-year-old McQueen plays a character barely past adolescence and thirsting for revenge. Co-starring with Karl Malden, Steve enjoyed the location filming, far from Los Angeles.

The same year, he starred in *The Sand Pebbles* directed by Robert Wise, which also featured one of his co-stars from *The Great Escape*, Richard Attenborough. The film was set during the Chinese civil wars of the 1920s; McQueen played chief engineer Jake Holman, who joins the gunboat USS *San Pablo*, assigned to patrol the Yangtze River. The largely Chinese coolies who operate the boat are hostile to this stranger who tries to take command. While Holman struggles with his crew's antipathy, the country erupts in bloody revolution, forcing the sailors into increasingly dangerous situations. A study in the consequences of decolonization and a critique of Western civilization, the film also gave McQueen the opportunity to play a grizzled veteran whose face showed all the marks of his years of service. 'Two or three times a day he'd say, 'I think I can get this across better without a line, with just an expression',' director Robert Wise recalled. 'The first couple of times I kept thinking, he's not giving me anything,' he continued. 'Then when I saw the rushes I was knocked out.' Steve's portrayal earned Best Actor nominations at the 1967 Oscars and Golden Globes. The film received Oscar nominations in eight categories and Richard Attenborough won a Golden Globe for Best Supporting Actor. There were no awards for McQueen but his career was at its peak. In 1968, he signed for almost $750,000 dollars to play Thomas Crown opposite Faye Dunaway in *The Thomas Crown Affair*, where he was reunited with his *Cincinnati Kid* director, Norman Jewison. 'He was so wired that half the time I didn't understand what he was saying,' remembered the director. Clips from the making of the film show McQueen addressing his director in rather surprising fashion: 'No. Listen to me. I'm doing the fucking film, so stop twisting my melon.'

Steve McQueen's range broadened with *The Thomas Crown Affair*, proving that he could play an upmarket businessman with as much ease and naturalness as his usual rebellious character. Thomas Crown was an elegant, chess-playing Boston Brahmin. Although the film was criticized for its 'staggeringly exhausting' shooting schedule, it was a huge popular success and subsequently became a classic. Thirty years later, in 1999, it was remade by John McTiernan who astonishingly cast Pierce Brosnan opposite the radiant Rene Russo, while Faye Dunaway took a cameo role as Crown's psychoanalyst.

Also in 1968, Steve McQueen played a Los Angeles cop in *Bullitt*, adapted from Robert L. Pike's novel *Mute Witness* and directed by Englishman Peter Yates. *Bullitt* is a police lieutenant selected by an ambitious politician to protect Johnny Ross, a gangster whose testimony is crucial to a hearing involving the politician. Despite the precautions taken by *Bullitt* and his men, Ross is seriously wounded and dies in hospital. *Bullitt* discovers that the victim isn't the real Ross …

Playing opposite Robert Vaughn, who also appeared in *The Magnificent Seven*, and co-star Jacqueline Bisset, McQueen gave a performance that made history. 'Steve is a marvellous actor,' said Peter Yates. 'After one or two takes, he said to me "Don't give me too much dialogue." His reactions, his eye movements were completely extraordinary. Watch his eyes.' Although McQueen's face often appears stoic, the actor knew how to express the essentials of his character by means of looks and silences. The critic Andrew Sarris expanded on this: 'He doesn't share everything, but he communicates something just the same. Some people are so numb from pain they're just blocks of wood. But he was very expressive. You can feel his pain.'

Bullitt had a tremendous impact on McQueen's career, thanks to the spectacular car chase through San Francisco and its suburbs. The scene became a classic of US cinema, one of the first high-speed car chases in cinema history. It stands out from those that followed because of its gripping realism, the result of clever camera angles and editing. In fact, for this scene Steve McQueen called in his friend Bill Hickman, a former motorcycle stuntman, to drive the car he followed in the film. Two Ford Mustangs and two Dodge Chargers were used and at times they reached speeds of 200 km (124 miles) per hour. The chase scene took three weeks to shoot.

The film marked a turning point in the way car chases were shot. Unlike the scenes in *Duel* (Steven Spielberg, 1971) or John Landis's *Blues Brothers* (1980), which used ordinary cars, *Bullitt*'s Ford Mustang Fastback V8 390 GT and the killers' Dodge Charger V8 440 were real racing cars. The object of the scene was not to demolish the greatest number of cars (as in *The Blues Brothers*) or to feature a lot of stunting, but to give a demonstration of sheer skill in driving. The gamble paid off, as posterity has proved.

The film, which was produced by McQueen, was a huge popular success and won the Oscar for best film editing. Steve McQueen chose British director Peter Yates because he had seen and liked *Robbery* (1967). Yates accepted, subject to changes in the script and on condition that filming took place on location, to update the story. As always, McQueen kept up the pressure on Warners but when shooting finished the studio terminated his five-film contract and in 1969 he signed a $20-million contract with CBS/Cinema Center. Like that of his characters, his self-sufficient style reached new heights.

In 1969 he starred in Mark Rydell's excellent *The Reivers*, adapted from a novel by William Faulkner. During shooting in Mississippi, Steve had numerous disagreements with Mark Rydell; nevertheless, the film was nominated in two categories for the Oscars and the Golden Globes, including a Best Actor nomination at the Golden Globes for McQueen.

The King of Cool?

Steve McQueen was the most highly paid actor of the 1960s and, while he was universally popular, he had a reputation for being difficult; in addition to his solitary nature and his notorious reputation for womanizing, he was famously capricious during shooting. 'I just don't know where he's coming from,' director Don Siegel once said. 'Every meeting he was late. Every fucking meeting he'd freak out. Where does he get off treating people this way? But you know what's the greatest tragedy to me? That shit's a great actor.' This opinion was shared by the great names of the period – for Frank Sinatra, McQueen was the best, and actor Edward G. Robinson told the press, 'He comes out of the tradition of Gable, Bogie, Cagney and even me. He's a stunner.' Yet McQueen doubted his talent as an actor: 'My range isn't very great; I have to find characters and situations that feel right,' he used to say. Nevertheless, he was equally seductive whether he adopted the ferocious stare of the poker-player in *The Cincinnati Kid*, the beaten-down look of the betrayed ex-con in *The Getaway* or the charming smile of the renegade millionaire in *The Thomas Crown Affair*. However, McQueen rarely received the praise showered on his peers and had few awards to show for his work. Was this relative lack of recognition due to his bad character?

One day he threatened publicly to break Howard Hughes's nose if Hughes didn't stop pestering the actress Mamie Van Doren, with whom both men had an affair, although not at the same time. Needless to say, Hughes never bothered Van Doren again. On some films, McQueen demanded the supply of electric razors and dozens of pairs of jeans. Later it was discovered that these caprices were in fact destined for Boys Republic, the remand home where he had spent more than a year in his youth. This orphan in search of an identity sometimes abused the power of his stardom. Although he worked hard, he also lived hard and did not mince his words. His reputation attracted attention and he featured simultaneously on 'Enemies Lists' compiled by Charles Manson and Richard Nixon.

Still obsessed with motor racing, he drove a Porsche 908 in a 12-hour endurance race at Sebring, California in 1970. Although driving with his leg in plaster after a motorcycle accident two weeks earlier, McQueen finished the course and he and his partner Peter Revson came second, 23 seconds after Mario Andretti in a Ferrari 512S. 'The only time I'm really relaxed is when going fast, in a car or a motorcycle,' the actor said. McQueen was passionate about motor sports, insisting on doing some of his own movie stunts, and this led to the 1971 film *Le Mans*, directed by Lee H. Katzin. The pitch was that Michael Delaney, racing driver, prepares to drive in the 24-hour Le Mans road race a year after a serious accident in which another driver, Pierre Belgetti, was killed. Delaney, driving a Porsche 917 sponsored by Gulf Oil, is one of the two course favourites with the German Erich Stahler, both watched by Lisa, Belgetti's widow.

McQueen took considerable risks with this film – stunt risks, obviously, but also financial risks, since his own company was producing it. The film retraces the 1970 Le Mans 24-hour race, which provided much of the footage. Steve McQueen was heavily involved in the shoot, which he considered the high point of his whole career. He planned to take part in the real Le Mans 24-hour race with Jackie Stewart as co-driver, but insurers refused to cover the risk and he wound up in the stands being filmed for crowd scenes. However, he managed to hire the circuit for three months in summer 1970 in order to recreate the course and the duels of the 25 racing cars he assembled, along with many drivers and mechanics. To finish the shots of the race, he had the thrill of driving himself. The lack of a script and the extravagant expenditure on the shooting led the director, John Sturges, and the editor, Ferris Webster, to quit due to the pressures of production. During filming, the ever-present danger created constant tension and director Lee H. Katzin took over under difficult conditions, as McQueen had been involved in a high-speed car crash; he escaped uninjured but driver David Piper lost a leg following a crash in his Porsche 917.

The semi-documentary film flopped at the box office and closed down McQueen's production company. However, *Le Mans* remains probably the best film ever made about motor racing, largely thanks to the quality of its camera angles.

Also in 1971, Steve McQueen made a documentary, *On Any Sunday*, about the world of biking, a world he loved as much as motor racing. 'I love racing of any kind,' he said 'because my name means nothing to the guy beside me. He only wants to beat me.' The documentary aimed to give the public a realistic picture of this little-known world. 'At the time,' McQueen explained, 'most biking films focused on its grungy, outlaw side, which is as far away from the world of bike racing as I am from Lionel Barrymore.'

A Seventies papillon (1972–4)

In 1972, Steve McQueen filmed *Junior Bonner*, an excellent film by Sam Peckinpah that shows the defeats of an ageing rodeo champion in decline. A careful character study, the film also won Steve the accolade of being made a member of the Association of Stuntmen, having himself performed most of the scenes on horseback, a performance that led to several injuries. But despite his bruises and his 42nd birthday, he didn't hesitate to appear with bare torso and seemed in great form on screen. Real rodeo scenes and genuine empathy for his role won him excellent reviews.

Again directed by Peckinpah, McQueen played Carter McCoy in *The Getaway*, a film that lightly sent up the traditional morals of film noir. In exchange for his freedom, prisoner Carter McCoy must rob a bank as soon as he gets out of prison. Double-crossed by his accomplice Rudy Butler, he goes on the run across the United States with his wife and the stolen money. The director indulged his usual fondness for ritual violence in this adaptation of Jim Thomson's noir novel, but the thriller basically relied on McQueen's performance, which would make it a classic. (It was remade more than 20 years later, starring Alec Baldwin and Kim Basinger.) His role of a crook trapped by his past as well as by his benefactor suited McQueen to perfection. This time, he played a very different con to Thomas Crown – a turncoat swindler and a shameless killer.

It was during this film that Steve McQueen met Ali MacGraw, who shared star billing with him although her acting did not gain equal enthusiasm from the critics. Ironically, it was Ali's husband, Paramount head of production Robert Evans, who landed the part for his wife; she soon fell for the seductive 40-something McQueen, who had separated from his first wife, Neile Adams, in 1970, divorcing her in 1972. A year later he married Ali, becoming stepfather to her son, Josh Evans, then aged two.

Throughout the 1970s McQueen remained the best-paid actor in the US. Always the King of Cool, even at the height of his fame he still frequented local eateries and registered as unemployed between movies. His laid-back style was genuine; to Steve, money was a source of freedom, not of riches.

In 1972, he joined First Artists, a company founded by Barbra Streisand, Paul Newman and Sidney Poitier to fund and distribute their own productions.

In 1973, McQueen played the title role in *Papillon*, directed by Franklin J. Schaffner from the best-seller by Henri Charrière. Filming proved difficult at times – Steve had many disagreements with his co-star Dustin Hoffman, who was also his associate at First Artists. As usual, Steve refused to use doubles for his stunts and was always ready to run through thick scrubland or fling himself into deep-sea manoeuvres.

Although the story underwent some adaptation, the film remained true to the novel and Steve McQueen gave an irreproachable, restrained performance alongside a brilliant Dustin Hoffman. The film, an indictment of penal colonies, allowed the actors to stretch their talents in a tough, poignant epic. McQueen showed himself in sombre guise playing the role of a prisoner. Few actors would dare to disguise themselves so unflatteringly on screen but McQueen didn't give a damn. His performance was a great critical and popular success and was nominated for a Golden Globe Award.

An 'infernal' superstar (1974–8)

In 1974 Steve joined Paul Newman, William Holden, Faye Dunaway and Fred Astaire in *The Towering Inferno*, directed by John Guillermin and Irwin Allen. Although the script was hardly original – a fire breaks out during the launch party for a colossal building, trapping the occupants in a glass tower – *The Towering Inferno* was a sweet deal for McQueen. The only problem was that he had to share billing with one of his rivals, Paul Newman.

In the original script, Steve's character had 12 fewer lines than Paul Newman's. McQueen insisted on the script being changed so that he had the same number of lines as Newman. He considered himself a better actor than Paul Newman and wanted the critics to judge the final result on equal ground. In the early 1970s Irwin Allen, co-director and producer of the film, specialized in spectacular disaster movies with lavish special effects, such as *The Poseidon Adventure*. At the time, disaster movies were hugely successful and *The Towering Inferno* caught the wave of 1970s super-productions – including *Jaws*, *The Exorcist*, *The Texas Chainsaw Massacre* and *Star Wars* – that saved the studios. While all these films were enormously successful, the production budget for *The Towering Inferno* was a record for the time. McQueen's role as the fire-chief also brought him his highest fee – $1 million upfront and 10 per cent of the gross.

For once, most of the stunts were done in the studio, but the flames were real and McQueen got close enough at times to smell the burning. As the courageous fire-chief, the 'Bandito' was the only watchable thing on screen. The film was a huge popular success and also garnered a fair number of awards. *The Towering Inferno* won Oscars for Best Cinematography, Best Film Editing and Best Music, Original Song (Al Kasha and Joel Hirschhorn, for 'We May Never Love Like This Again'). It was also nominated for Best Picture, Best Actor in a Supporting Role (Fred Astaire), Best Art Direction-Set Decoration (William J. Creber, Ward Preston and Raphael Bretton), Best Music, Original Dramatic Score (John Williams) and, finally, Best Sound (Theodore Soderberg and Herman Lewis). The success of the film didn't stop there; it also won a Golden Globe for Best Supporting Actor (Fred Astaire) and for Most Promising Newcomer (Susan Flannery), plus 1976 BAFTA awards for Best Film Music and Best Supporting Actor (Fred Astaire), while in Japan it won the 1976 Kinema Junpo Award for Best Foreign Film.

Worldwide, the film made a profit of $80 million, and McQueen allowed himself to go into semi-retirement in Malibu.

Following the huge success of *The Towering Inferno*, Steve announced that any producer who wanted to work with him had to send a cheque for $1½ million along with the script. If he liked the screenplay and wanted to make the film, he would cash the cheque; the producer would then owe him another $1½ million. He would keep half of his $3 million salary if the producer was unable or unwilling to give him the other half. 'Pay-or-play' was what a producer had to do if he wanted McQueen in his movie. He used this unprecedented behaviour to ensure the six-and-a-half years of semi-retirement that he took after *The Towering Inferno*. Apart from an uncredited appearance in a biker movie called *Dixie Dynamite*, Steve did not make another film until 1978, when he played Dr Stockmann in *An Enemy of the People*, directed by George Schaefer.

Following the success of *The Towering Inferno*, *The Blob* was re-released during the 1970s in an attempt to cash in on the vogue for disaster movies.

Calm after the storm: Santa Paula (1978–80)

Steve McQueen turned down many screenplays before deciding to return to the screen. Adapted from an Ibsen play, *An Enemy of the People* was one project he cared about – he decided to act in the film and even to be executive producer because of what he saw as its ecological message. 'The theme ties right in to the problems we face today with polluted lakes and poisoned air and chemicals in all our food. That's what attracted me to this play, the message it carries – that we need to take personal responsibility for what's happening around us. That's what Ibsen was saying.' To play the country doctor reviled for his political convictions, McQueen grew a beard and let his hair grow. He also put on a lot of weight. Rumours were rife, including hints of drugs and sickness. The film was poorly received by critics and public; fans and journalists were disappointed not to see the McQueen they expected.

In 1979, Steve McQueen changed his life. Having divorced Ali McGraw in 1978, he now had a new fiancée, Barbara Minty, a young model 17 years his junior. He learned to fly and the FAA allowed him to take out a private pilot's licence although he was nearly 50. He abandoned his sumptuous residences in Brentwood and Malibu for a ranch in Santa Paula on the outskirts of Los Angeles and spent his time riding his motorcycle collection and flying an old crate, just like his father, the former stunt pilot.

On 16 January 1980, Barbara Minty became Steve's third wife. Under her influence and that of his aviation instructor, Sammy Mason, the King of Cool became almost conservative and turned to religion, specifically Evangelical or 'born again' Christianity.

In 1980, he played Tom Horn in the film of the same name, directed by William Wiard and co-starring Linda Evans. McQueen was also executive producer of the film and spent months getting back into shape after *An Enemy of the People*. As Tom Horn, he took on the character of an archetypal hero of the Old West. After two studio films, he was pleased to be shooting on location but his health wasn't good and during filming he started to have breathing problems. In fact, cancer was taking a hold – these respiratory ailments were the first symptoms of lung cancer, which was diagnosed between 1979 and 1980; but McQueen kept his illness secret.

Also in 1980, he starred as Ralph Thorson in *The Hunter*, directed by Buzz Kulik. His fee was $5 million and 15 per cent of the gross. The film was part psychological study, part action movie and Steve played with brio the bounty hunter who was both cop and outlaw. It was his last role.

Preoccupied with his cancer and the poor prognosis from American doctors, Steve decided to undergo experimental treatments in Mexico.

Steve McQueen died in Juárez, Mexico in the early hours of 7 November 1980; at 3.45 a.m. he had a heart attack, following an operation to remove the mesothelioma (cancer) that had developed. He was 50. The causes of his death are still obscure.

It was long thought that he had died of cancer contracted through asbestos in the fireproof clothing he wore while motor racing. However, there were suspicions of poor hygiene and security in the clinic where he was operated on and his doctor claimed he had been injected with a fatal coagulant the evening before he died.

McQueen was cremated, leaving a question mark hanging over the true circumstances of his death, and his ashes were scattered in the Pacific Ocean.

In 1982, his extensive collection of cars and motorcycles was auctioned off, along with the plane he had bought shortly before his death.

After his death, a commemorative plaque was placed on the wall outside Boys Republic reformatory. It read 'When Steve McQueen arrived here, he was a troubled boy; when he left, he was a man. Although he was a great film star, he often came back to tell us about himself and his success. His example is a source of hope and inspiration for our pupils now and in the future.' Of hope, that's the least that could be said. A few years before he became an actor, Steve McQueen was a young delinquent. A few years before he became a movie star, Steve McQueen was a runner in a brothel. A few years before his fee was $5 million and a percentage of the gross, Steve McQueen raced cars on the last weekend of every month – and more than 25 years after his death he still inspires advertisers, publishers and directors.

A living legend

Steve McQueen's last words were 'I did it'. We can imagine that the phrase with which he expressed his satisfaction at having survived an operation applied equally to the rest of his life. But the story is far from over.

More than 25 years after his death, he remains a superstar. Thanks to DVDs, we can still admire the intrepid soldier of *The Great Escape*, the implacable cop of *Bullitt*, the bounty hunter in the 94 episodes of *Wanted: Dead or Alive*, or the doctor and environmental champion from *An Enemy of the People*.

Despite a filmography of varying quality, McQueen knew throughout his career how to project a personality at once disconcerting and seductive. There were few films of the highest quality in his career but when he was in one Steve McQueen always rose to the heights, as can be seen in Mark Rydell's *The Reivers* (1969) or Sam Peckinpah's *Junior Bonner* (1972). By making judicious choices such as *Bullitt*, *Papillon* or *Tom Horn*, Steve McQueen knew how to create memorable characters whose roots were profoundly anchored to the American psyche of the time.

Steve McQueen's legacy survives. In 1988, Chuck Russell remade *The Blob* with Kevin Dillon; in 1995, *Empire* magazine cited McQueen as one of the hundred sexiest stars in cinema history; he came 66th in an *Entertainment Weekly* poll of all-time great actors and 33rd in a similar poll by *Première*. In 1994, Alec Baldwin recreated his role in *The Getaway* and Pierce Brosnan played Thomas Crown in 1999. Even now, more than 25 years after his death, there are statues and 6-metre (20-foot) high frescoes of him. Thanks to digital technology, he was shown behind the wheel of a new Mustang for an advertising campaign. Absolut Vodka featured him as 'The Absolute Man' in a recent publicity campaign and Sheryl Crow even won a Grammy Award for a tribute song. All things that would doubtless make him smile or yell, like his character Henri Charrière in *Papillon*: 'Hey, you bastards. I'm still here!'

Not many people knew the man, even fewer knew the actor. He rarely, if ever, confided in others. He loved to say 'Nobody trusts anybody. Otherwise, why would anyone twist your melons?' The man was full of paradoxes – fanatically loyal but totally paranoid, devoted but unfaithful, a free spirit in search of legitimacy, internationally famous yet desperate for anonymity and solitude. 'I've done everything one can do on earth, but I've wrecked most of my life,' he wrote. Undoubtedly it's these ambiguities that made Steve McQueen such an attractive actor and still make him an outstanding personality of our age. For, while he doubted his range as an actor, McQueen never doubted his stature. History has proved him right – as a movie icon reaching across time and generations, his image is timeless and his aura still shines.

«I took up acting because I wanted to beat the 40 hour-a-week rap. But I didn't escape because now I'm working 72 hours a week. So there you go.»

Steve McQueen

1957/For three years, Steve McQueen played a bounty-hunter in the TV series *Wanted: Dead or Alive*. It was his first big screen part.

1959/The television series
Wanted: Dead or Alive brought
Steve McQueen fame and
recognition. He was 29.
From then on, he was offered
leading roles in movies.

1959/ Poster for *Never So Few*, directed by John Sturges. The film was shot in the actual locations where the story took place, in Burma and Cambodia.

1959/Frank Sinatra, George Peppard and Steve McQueen in *Never So Few*.

1961/A portrait of Steve McQueen aged 31, while filming *The Honeymoon Machine*.

1961/Steve McQueen and Julie Fitch in *The Honeymoon Machine* directed by Richard Thorpe. It was the only comedy he made.

1962/Shirley Anne Field and Steve McQueen, the stars of Philip Leacock's *The War Lover.*

1962/Filming of *The War Lover* took place in England. Steve McQueen stayed at the Savoy, getting into trouble with the hotel's management because he organized memorable parties and races down the corridors.

«My childhood was the worst shit you could imagine.»

Steve McQueen

1960/Steve McQueen at home in Hollywood.

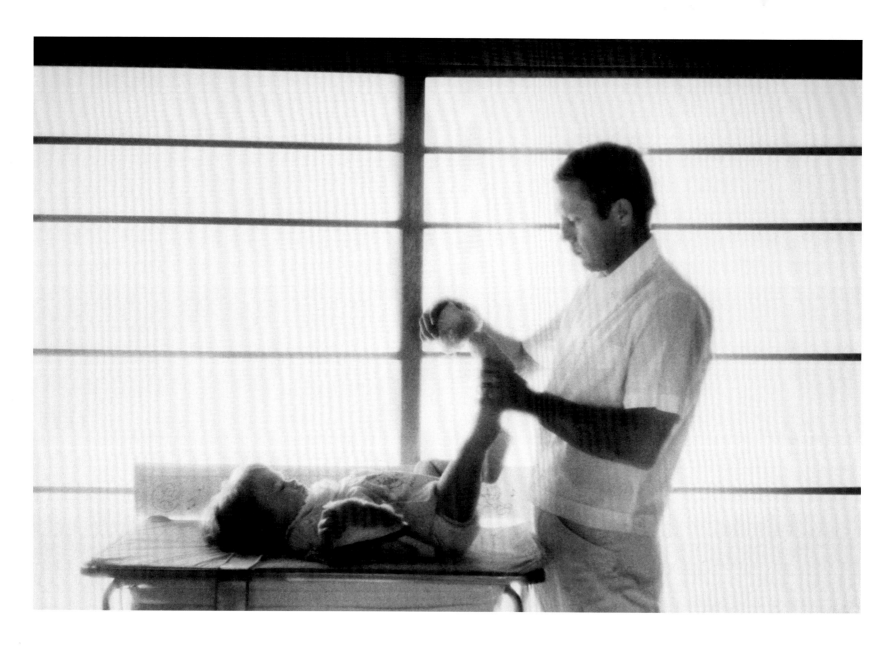

1960/Steve McQueen changes his daughter, Terry, in his house on Solar Drive, Hollywood.

1960/Family breakfast for Steve, his wife Neile and their daughter Terry.

1961/Proud father Steve McQueen with his son Chad.

1961/Steve McQueen
with his son Chad.

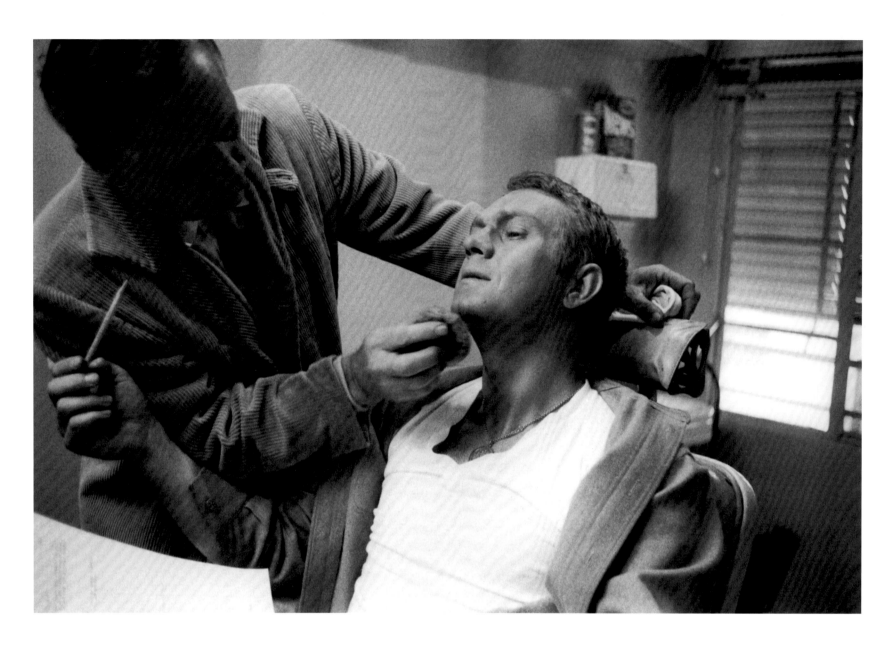

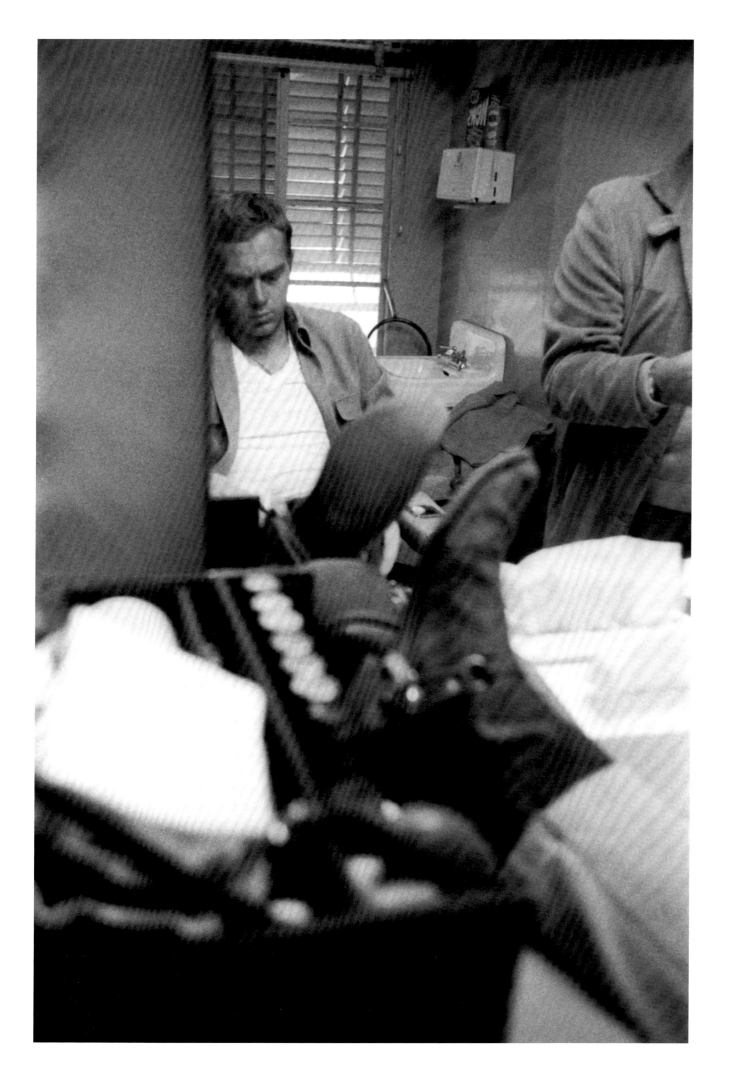

« I don't know why it (fame) happened – but it's kinda nice. Maybe it's because I'm someone off the streets. Maybe people relate to me. »

Steve McQueen

Previous pages:
1960/A fiendish poker game between the actors of *The Magnificent Seven*: Brad Dexter, Steve McQueen, James Coburn, Horst Buchholz, Yul Brynner.

40

1972/Steve McQueen at 42.

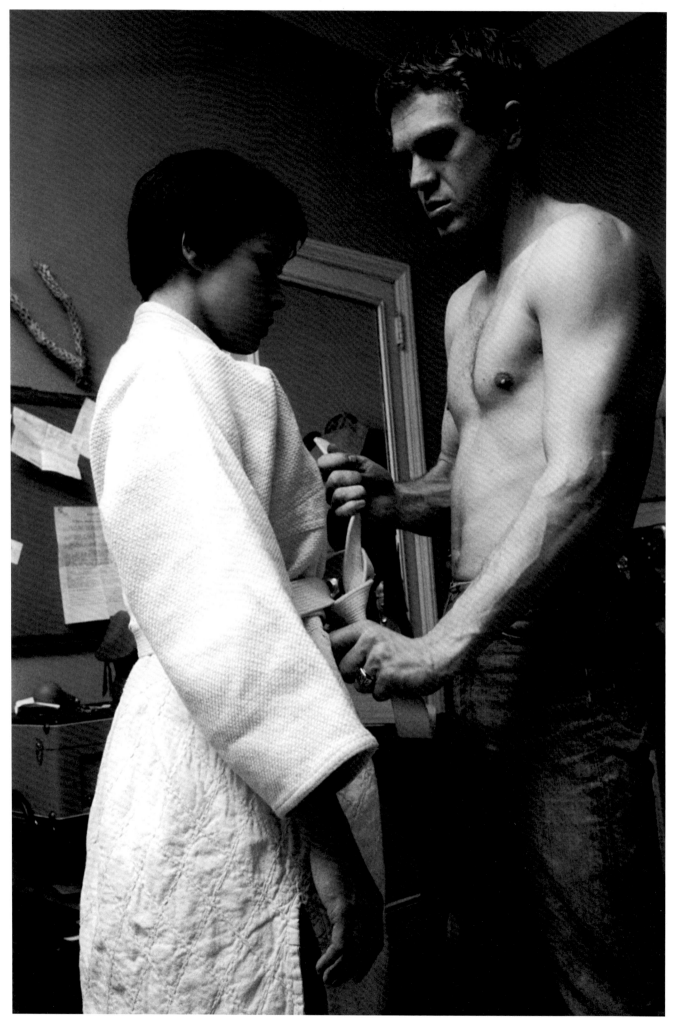

1957/Steve McQueen gives
a judo lesson to his wife Neile.

42

1957/Steve McQueen introduces his wife Neile to judo.

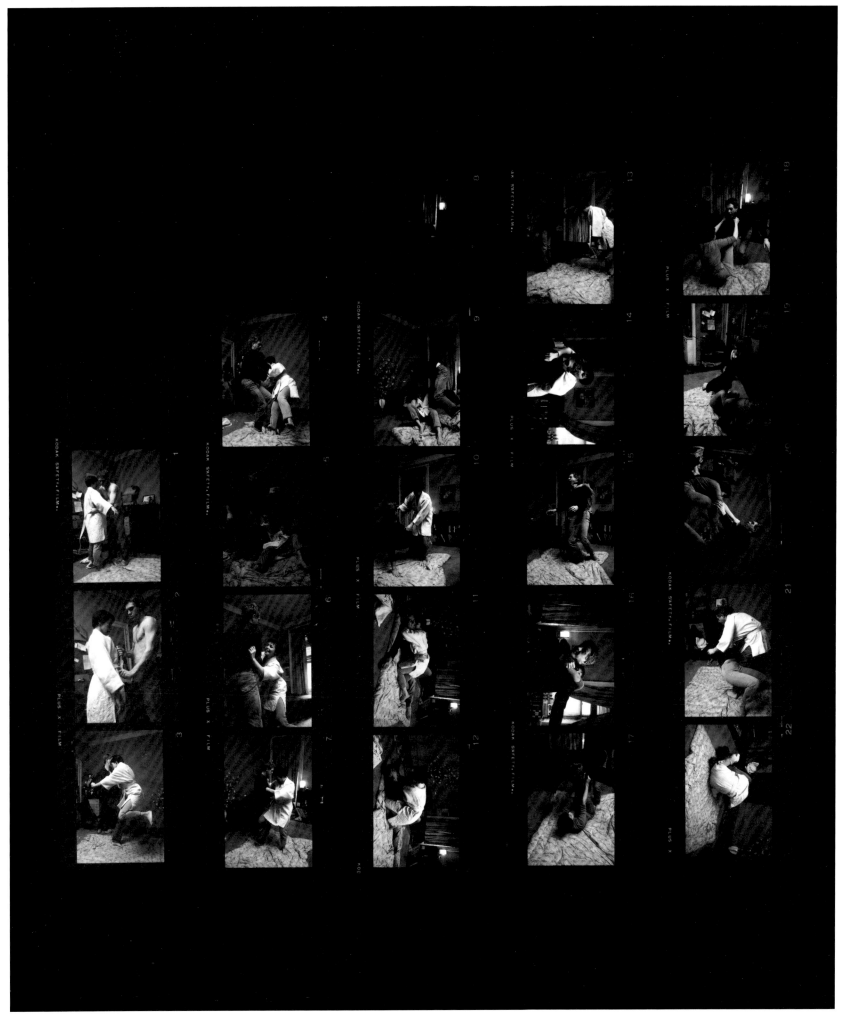

1960/Steve McQueen, his wife Neile and their daughter Terry in front of their house in the Hollywood Hills.

1960/Steve McQueen shows his Jaguar XKSS to director John Sturges on the Metro Goldwyn Mayer studios parking lot, Hollywood.

1961/Steve McQueen and his mechanic.

«When I believe in something, I fight like hell for it.»

Steve McQueen

1959/Steve McQueen in
his Porsche Speedster on
the Riverside Raceway circuit.

1961/Steve McQueen gets ready to go round the circuit at the wheel of his Lotus Eleven.

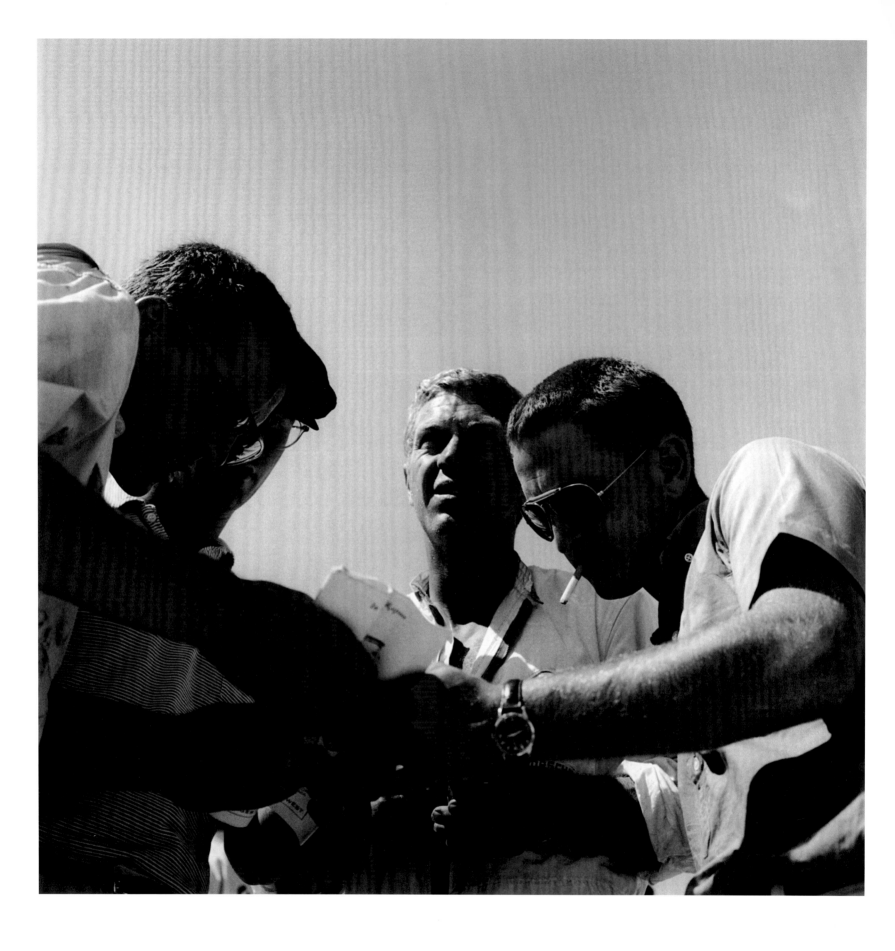

1960/Steve McQueen and his mechanics make last-minute adjustments to his vehicle before going round the circuit.

1961/Steve McQueen prepares for road racing.

« I enjoy racing in any form because the guy next to me couldn't care less what my name is. He just wants to beat me. »

Steve McQueen

1960/ Steve McQueen makes final preparations before a race.

1961/Steve McQueen at the wheel of his Lotus Eleven.

« Steve is a marvellous actor. His reactions, his eye movements are just extraordinary. Just watch his eyes! »

Peter Yates, Director

1963/Steve McQueen aged 33, while making *The Great Escape*, directed by John Sturges.

64

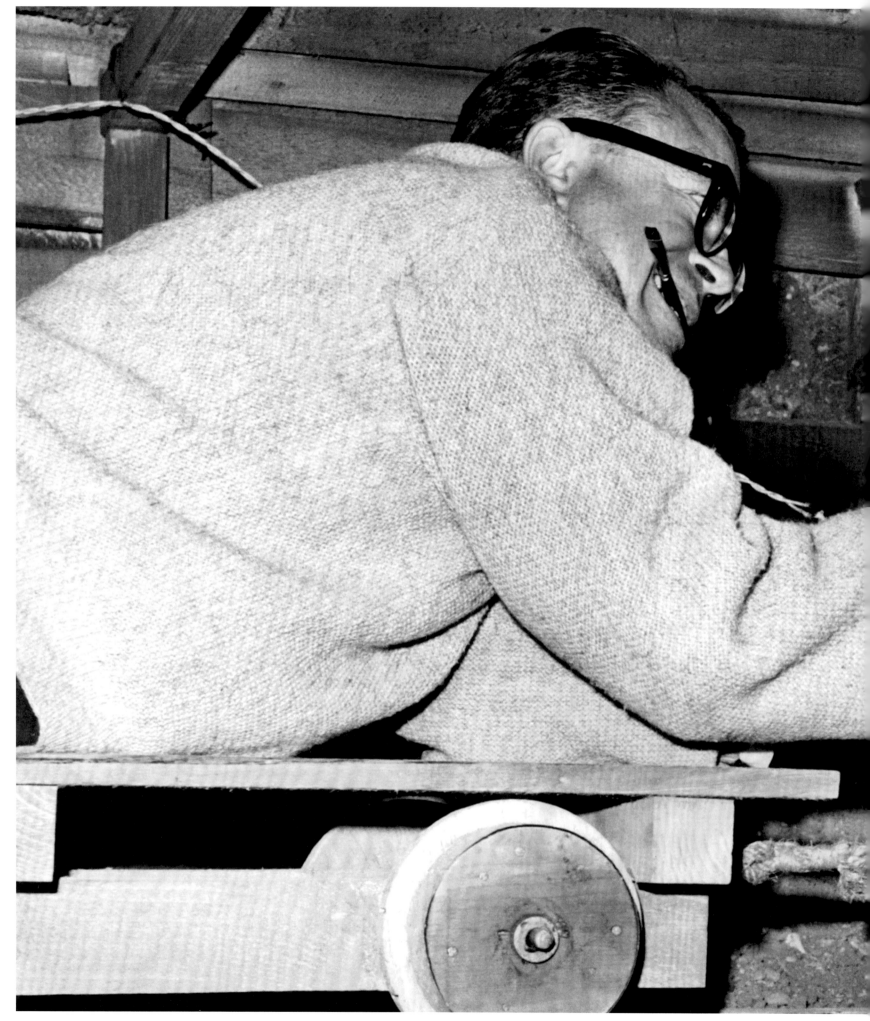

Previous pages:
1963/Steve McQueen's make-up is retouched during the shooting of *The Great Escape*.

1963/While filming *The Great Escape*, Steve McQueen gave director John Sturges and the producers a hard time, as he wanted to do all his own motorbike stunts – until the film's insurers refused.

«Everything he does is authentic.»

George Cukor, Director

1967/Steve McQueen, aged 37.

1960/Steve McQueen, his wife Neile, and their dog Mike.

1960/Steve McQueen at home on the Hollywood Heights.

1960/Steve, his wife Neile, and their dog Mike in their Hollywood Hills home.

1960/Steve McQueen plays with his dog Mike.

1960/Steve McQueen and his son Chad.

«I had neither a mother's love nor a father's authority.»

Steve McQueen

1960/Steve McQueen
and his son Chad.

Previous pages:
1960/Steve McQueen driving his
Jaguar XK SS at top speed around
Nichols Canyon, California.

1960/Steve McQueen lunches
with producers.

« Most actors get big-headed. I don't want to be like that, and I'm not vain enough to think that I'm an exception. »

Steve McQueen

1968/Steve McQueen on the set of *Bullitt*, directed by Peter Yates.

1967/A fitting with his tailor.

1963/Steve McQueen in his agent's office.

«Acting's a hard scene for me. Every script I get is an enemy I have to conquer.»

Steve McQueen

Previous pages:
1965/Steve McQueen lends his support to Braude Circa, a candidate for mayor of Los Angeles, at his campaign HQ.

1966/Taken on the set of *Nevada Smith*.

96

1960/While filming *Wanted: Dead or Alive*, Steve McQueen organized gambling parties to lighten the atmosphere between takes.

68

67

66

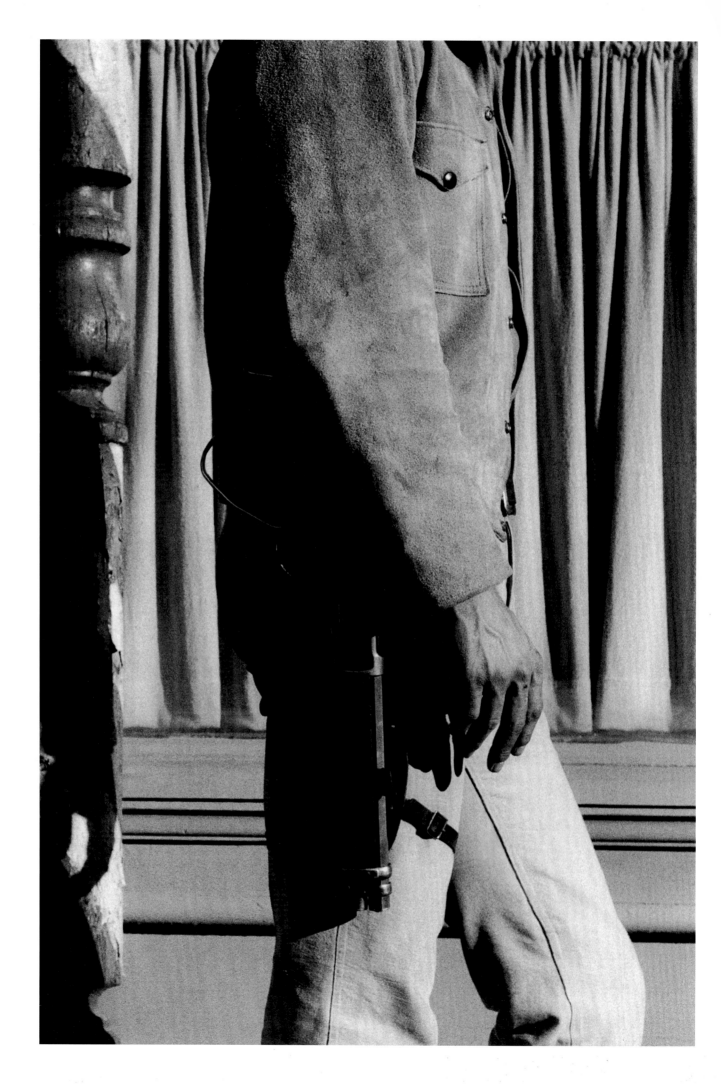

1960 / Steve McQueen in the TV series *Wanted: Dead or Alive*.

1960/A portrait taken on the set of *Wanted: Dead or Alive.*

«I live for myself and I answer to nobody.»

Steve McQueen

1968/During the filming of *Bullitt.*

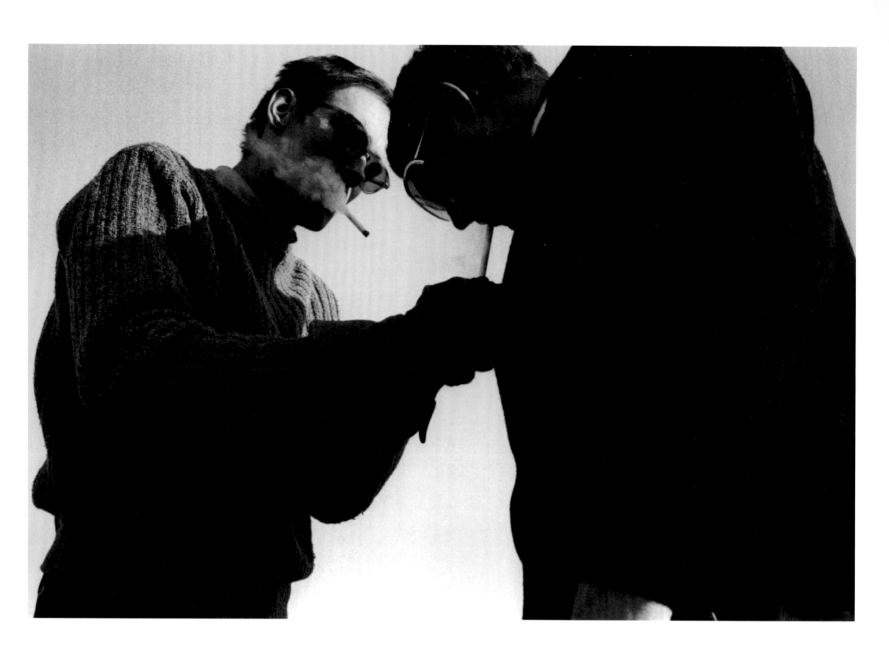

1960/Steve McQueen and a friend about to test their bikes in the sand dunes.

1961/Steve McQueen was an experienced driver. When he was a student at the Actors Studio, he went motor racing to make some extra money.

1961/Steve McQueen and
a friend go cross-country.

« I'm not sure that acting is something for a grown man to be doing. »

Steve McQueen

1969/Taken on the set of
The Reviers, inspired by a novel
by William Faulkner and directed
by Mark Rydell.

1966 /Steve McQueen on the set of *The Sand Pebbles*, directed by Robert Wise.

1967/Steve McQueen gained a Best Actor Oscar nomination for his role in *The Sand Pebbles*. His co-star, Marayat Andrian (Emmanuelle Arsan), became famous some years later, as the author of the bestseller *Emmanuelle*.

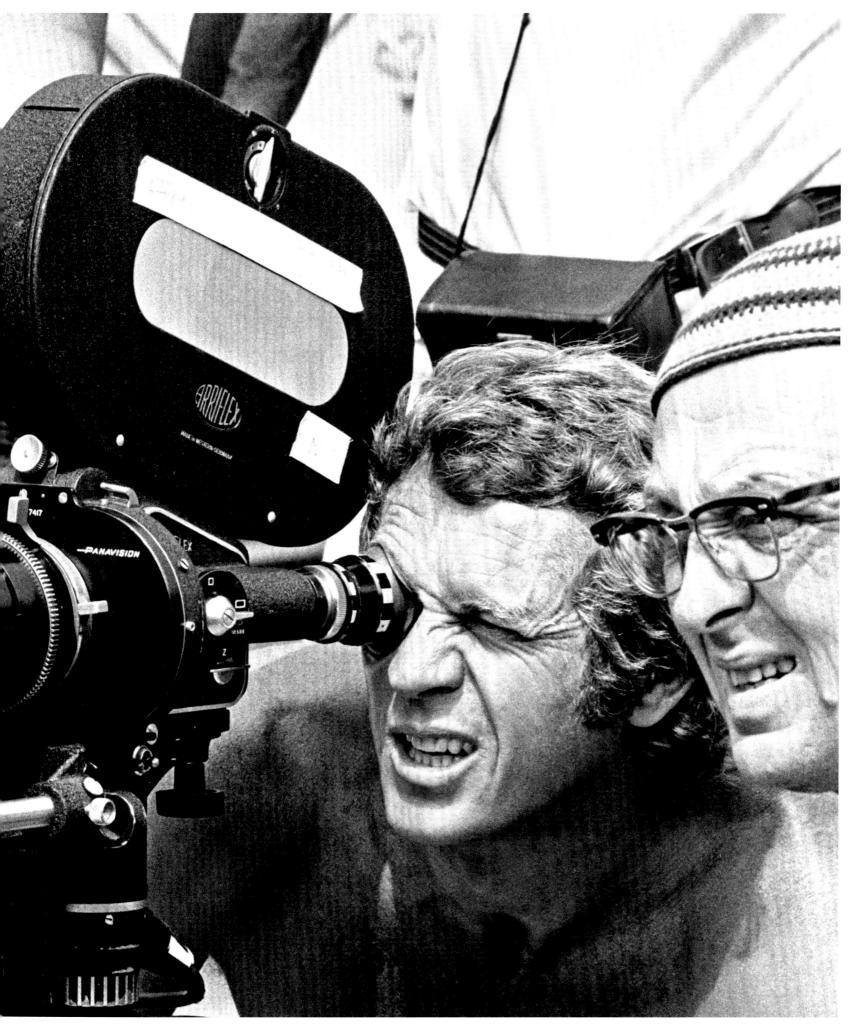

« I'm out of the Midwest. It was a good place to come from. It gives you a sense of right or wrong and fairness, which is lacking in our society. »

Steve McQueen

Previous pages:
1971/Steve McQueen and the director Lee H. Katzin filming *Le Mans*.

118

1969/Photographed on the set of *The Reivers*, directed by Mark Rydell. McQueen was 39 at the time.

Previous pages:
1967/Steve and his wife Neile
pose in front of their house,
seated on their Ferrari 275 GTS.

1970/Steve and his wife
Neile at home.

1965/Steve and his wife Neile at home in Hollywood.

«I worked hard, and if you work hard you get the goodies.»

Steve McQueen

Previous pages:
1966/Steve McQueen and his wife Neile at the première of *The Sand Pebbles*.

128

1966/Steve McQueen with his Ferrari 250GT Lusso. The car was auctioned by Christies in 2007 for a record-breaking $2.3 million.

1967/Steve McQueen and Nathalie Wood at the Golden Globe Awards. The actor was nominated as Best Actor for *Love with the Proper Stranger*.

1966/Accompanied by his wife Neile, Steve McQueen leaves his hand and footprints on Hollywood Boulevard in front of Grauman's Chinese Theater.

«Acting's a good racket. And let's face it, you can't beat it for the bread.»

Steve McQueen

1968/On the set of *The Thomas Crown Affair.*

1968/In *The Thomas Crown Affair*, Steve McQueen played a sophisticated millionaire who robs banks. His role was reprised in 1999 by Pierce Brosnan. Faye Dunaway appeared in both versions.

1967/Steve and his wife Neile in their Mercedes Excalibur.

1968/Faye Dunaway and Steve McQueen in *The Thomas Crown Affair*.

«Stardom equals freedom. That's the only equation that matters.»

Steve McQueen

1968/The kiss scene between Faye Dunaway and Steve McQueen in *The Thomas Crown Affair* is the longest in cinema history.

138

WARNER BROS - SEVEN ARTS PRÉSENTE

STEVE McQUEEN

"BULLITT"

UNE PRODUCTION SOLAR

ROBERT VAUGHN
JACQUELINE BISSET
DON GORDON
ROBERT DUVALL
SIMON OAKLAND
NORMAN FELL
TECHNICOLOR®

d'après le roman "MUTE WITNESS" de ROBERT L. PIKE   mise en scène de PETER YATES   produit par PHILIP d'ANTONI
producteur exécutif ROBERT E. RELYEA   musique de LALO SCHIFRIN   scénario d'ALAN R. TRUSTMAN et HARRY KLEINER

1968/Poster for *Bullitt*, directed by Peter Yates, which gained seven nominations in various festivals, including the 1969 Oscar for Best Picture.

1968/The Ford Mustang Fastback GT 390 became a legend thanks to the film *Bullitt*, in which Steve McQueen drove it in a hair-raising car chase through the streets of San Francisco.

« Motor racing is the most exciting thing there is. But unlike drugs, you get high with dignity. »

Steve McQueen

Previous pages:
1959, Steve McQueen in *The Great St Louis Bank Robbery*, directed by Charles Guggenheim.

144

1970/A portrait taken while filming *Le Mans*, directed by Lee H. Katzin, released in 1971.

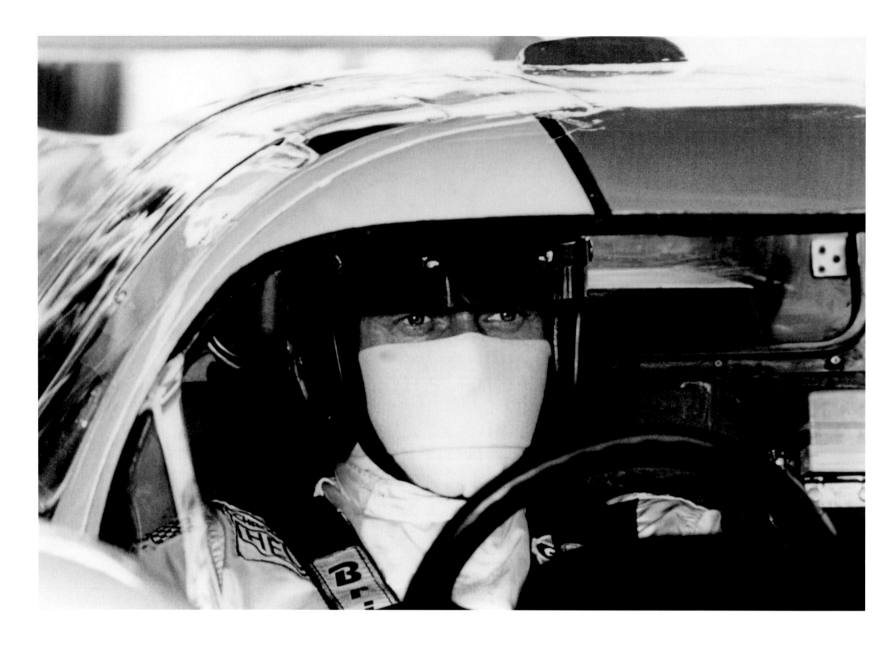

1970/Several pilots and stuntmen were seriously wounded during the early days of filming *Le Mans*, directed by Lee H. Katzin.

1970/Much of the film *Le Mans* was shot in real time during the 1970 24-hour Le Mans road race.

1970/Ali McGraw, heroine of *Love Story*, and Steve McQueen were one of the best-known couples of the 1970s.

1963/Steve McQueen at 33.

Previous pages:
1972/Ali McGraw and Steve McQueen in their Ferrari 250GT Lusso.

1972/Steve McQueen and Ali McGraw in *The Getaway*. The two actors married a year later.

« I just want the pine trees and my kids and the green grass. I want to get rich and fat and watch my children grow. »

Steve McQueen

1973/Poster for Franklin Schaffner's *Papillon*, which earned Steve a Golden Globe nomination for Best Motion Picture Actor – Drama. The film's only Oscar was for Best Music.

1973/Dustin Hoffman and Steve McQueen in *Papillon*. Often dressed simply in pyjamas for his role as a prisoner, McQueen fell seriously ill due to the ambient damp in his cell.

1973/Steve McQueen in Franklin Schaffner's *Papillon*, filmed in Spain and Jamaica.

1973/While filming *Papillon* in Jamaica, Steve McQueen made a deal with the celebrated paparazzo Ron Galella: he would allow him a ten-minute photo session on condition he left the island immediately. He didn't want pictures of his new relationship with Ali McGraw to appear in the tabloids.

1978/In *An Enemy of the People*, directed by George Schaefer, Steve McQueen astonished in a role that was the antithesis of his Hollywood star image.

1978/A realistic portrait taken during filming of George Schaefer's *An Enemy of the People*. Although the film was poorly distributed, it was shown at the American Film Festival in Deauville, France, 1978.

« An actor is a puppet, manipulated by a dozen other people. »

Steve McQueen

1974/Steve McQueen played the fire chief in *The Towering Inferno*. This disaster movie, whose budget was a record $14 million, earned $20 million in its first month in the United States before going on to worldwide success.

Previous pages:

1974/A photo of the leading actors in John Guillermin's *The Towering Inferno*: Robert Wagner, Fred Astaire, Richard Chamberlain, Paul Newman, William Holden, Faye Dunaway, Steve McQueen, Jennifer Jones, O.J. Simpson and Robert Vaughn.

1974/Poster for *The Towering Inferno*, directed by John Guillermin.

1975/Steve McQueen, Faye Dunaway and Paul Newman in *The Towering Inferno*. The film won three Oscars: Best Cinematography, Best Film Editing and Best Music, Original Song.

« If I hadn't made it as an actor, I might have wound up a hood. »

Steve McQueen

1980/Poster for *Tom Horn*, directed by William Wiard.

1980/Steve McQueen as the cowboy *Tom Horn*, in his penultimate film, which chronicled the decline of the Old West.

1972/Steve McQueen while filming *Junior Bonner*, directed by Sam Peckinpah.

«I've done everything there is to do, but a lot of my life was wasted.»

Steve McQueen

1970/Steve McQueen and his motorcycle collection.

1964/Steve McQueen at the wheel.

November 7, 1980

Steve McQueen dies at the age of 50.

Significant dates

1930	Terence Steven McQueen is born on 24 March, in Indiana.
1945	Sent to reform school, he leaves on his 16th birthday and enrols in the merchant navy.
1945–1946	Leaves the merchant navy and drifts through Texas, North Carolina and Canada, working as a driller, logger, amateur boxer.
1947–1950	Joins the Marines, aged 17. Working on a punishment detail, he is exposed to high levels of asbestos when stripping out a ship's boiler-room. He behaves heroically when saving five men from drowning, and returns to civilian life.
1950–1951	Settles in Greenwich Village, New York. Works at various jobs, including driving taxis, delivering newspapers, repairing TVs.
1952	Enrols in Sanford Meisner's acting classes at the Neighborhood Playhouse.
1952–1955	Gets a scholarship to the Actors Studio. Goes motor-racing at the end of every month.
1954	Plays the fourth lead in *The Shrivingon Raiders*.
1956	For several performances he plays the lead in *A Hatful of Rain* on Broadway. Gets a part in *Somebody Up There Likes Me*, where he meets Paul Newman for the first time. Marries Neile Adams in California.
1957–1960	Plays a bounty-hunter in *Wanted Dead or Alive*, a role that brings him fame and a regular income.
1959	Birth of his daughter Terry.
1960	First legendary role, in *The Magnificent Seven*. Birth of his son Chad.
1961	Signs a contract for $300,000 dollars and profit participation for *Soldier in the Rain*. Sets up his own production company, Solar Productions.
1962	Plays a leading role in *The Great Escape*.
1964	Nominated for a Golden Globe Award for *Love with the Proper Stranger*. Stops working for 18 months to devote himself to car and motorbike racing.
1967	Oscar nomination for *The Sand Pebbles*. Wins the Golden Globes Henrietta Award for World Film Favourite – Male. Signs $750,000 contract for *The Thomas Crown Affair*.
1969	Signs a $20 million contract with CBS/Cinema Center.
1970	Separates from his wife Neile. Nominated for a Golden Globe Award for his playing against type in *The Reivers*.
1972	Joins First Artists, founded by Paul Newman, Sidney Poitier and Barbara Streisand.
1973	Marries Ali McGraw. Oscar nomination for *Papillon*.
1974–1975	*The Towering Inferno* is a huge success. From now on, Steve McQueen fixes his price at $3 million and goes into semi-retirement in Malibu.
1978	Critics hate *An Enemy of the People*. The film is a commercial disaster.
1979	Signs a contract for $3 million plus 15% of the gross for *The Hunter*.
1979	Settles in a ranch at Santa Paula with his new fiancée, Barbara Minty, having divorced Ali McGraw. Shortly before Christmas, doctors diagnose advanced cancer, probably due to his exposure to asbestos.
1980	Goes to Mexico for experimental treatments and the removal of two tumours. He dies following two heart-attacks on 7 November.

Filmography

1953	*Girl on the Run*, directed by Arthur J. Beckhard (bit part, uncredited)
1956	*Somebody Up There Likes Me*, directed by Robert Wise
1858	*Never Love a Stranger*, directed by Robert Stevens
1958	*The Blob*, directed by Irvin S. Yeaworth Jr.
1959	*The Great St Louis Bank Robbery*, directed by Charles Guggenheim
1959	*Never So Few*, directed by John Sturges
1960	*The Magnificent Seven*, directed by John Sturges
1961	*The Honeymoon Machine*, directed by Richard Thorpe
1962	*Hell is for Heroes*, directed by Don Siegel
1962	*The War Lover*, directed by Philip Leacock
1963	*The Great Escape*, directed by John Sturges
1963	*Soldier in the Rain*, directed by Ralph Nelson
1963	*Love with the Proper Stranger*, directed by Robert Mulligan
1965	*Baby, the Rain Must Fall*, directed by Robert Mulligan
1965	*The Cincinnati Kid*, directed by Norman Jewison
1966	*Nevada Smith*, directed by Henry Hathaway
1966	*The Sand Pebbles*, directed by Robert Wise
1968	*The Thomas Crown Affair*, directed by Norman Jewison
1968	*Bullitt*, directed by Peter Yates
1969	*The Reivers*, directed by Mark Rydell
1971	*Le Mans*, directed by Lee H. Katzin
1971	*On Any Sunday*, directed by Bruce Brown
1972	*Junior Bonner*, directed by Sam Peckinpah
1972	*The Getaway*, directed by Sam Peckinpah
1973	*Papillon*, directed by Franklin J. Schaffner
1974	*The Towering Inferno*, directed by John Guillermin
1976	*Dixie Dynamite*, directed by Lee Frost (uncredited role)
1978	*An Enemy of the People*, directed by George Schaefer
1980	*Tom Horn*, directed by William Wiard
1980	*The Hunter*, directed by Buzz Kulik

Acknowledgements

Jérôme, Thomas, Pierre-Alexis, this is your book.
Thank you for having come from afar to help with this project.
You are special friends indeed...
never change, we love you the way you are!

I would also like to thank

Renaud Sauteret, for the commitment, enthusiasm
and humour that he brought to the project with his design.

Carmen Masi, Barbara Moore and Catherine Terk
for their invaluable help in researching the images.

And everyone who helps to make YB Éditions
such a pleasurable experience on an everyday basis,
even if just with their encouragement and support.

Yann-Brice Dherbier.

Picture Credits